ANCHORED IN FAITH – A SINGLE MOTHER'S JOURNEY

Latoya Glover

Paperback ISBN: 978-1-64873-525-7
Ebook ISBN: 978-1-64873-526-4

Published By Writers Publishing House
writerspublishinghouse.com

CONTENTS

DEDICATION

To all the single mothers who fight daily battles, often unseen, with unwavering strength, resilience, and love—this book is for you. May you find comfort, hope, and a reminder that you are never alone on this journey.

To my parents and family, thank you for the countless ways you have lifted me, supported me, and given me the strength to keep going. Your love and assistance have been a constant light in my life.

And to those who came into my life for a reason, though only for a season, thank you. Your presence, even if brief, taught me valuable lessons and shaped me in ways I carry forward. Each of you has played a part in this story, and for that, I am grateful.

With all my heart, thank you.

INTRODUCTION

Becoming a single mother isn't a path most envision, let alone choose. For many of us, it begins quietly, almost as if life redirects us when we're not looking—circumstances shifting, doors closing, decisions taking shape before we even know the weight of them. As a single mother of three, I've learned the contours of this terrain, not from some map, but through the raw experience of walking it every day. My story is one of thousands, a thread woven into the larger tapestry of single motherhood. Each thread is a testament to the quiet strength and unyielding resilience of women who keep pushing forward despite the odds.

The first battlefront, for many of us, is financial. There's a moment when you realize the math won't work. When child support checks stop arriving or were never part of the picture, everything sharpens. Rent, groceries, school supplies—each becomes a calculated decision, a negotiation with reality. I've stood in grocery aisles, weighing the difference between buying what's healthy and cheap, balancing my children's needs against the unyielding limits of a bank balance. It's a dance of stretching every dollar, knowing that an unexpected car repair or a sick day at work could tip the entire balance of the month.

Yet, it's more than just numbers. The absence of financial stability seeps into the fabric of daily life, casting long shadows. A missed school trip, a year without new shoes, another holiday with only the simplest gifts—these aren't just choices. They're sacrifices. And with each one comes that quiet voice whispering, "Am I enough? Am I failing them?" Guilt, like an unwanted companion, settles in the spaces between what we can do and what we wish we could.

Beyond the financial strain lies the sheer exhaustion—physical, mental, and emotional. Parenting alone is like running a marathon without a finish line in sight. There's no one to hand off to when your body aches or when you're battling the flu and your child has a fever at 2 a.m. The house doesn't clean itself, meals don't cook themselves, and no one else will explain fractions or tie shoelaces. Every cry, every question, every need—yours to handle. I've found myself hunched over the kitchen table late at night, too tired to move, but knowing the laundry still waits, school forms need signing, and tomorrow it all starts again.

And then there's the weight of decisions. You're the only voice in the room. When it's time to discipline, there's no one to back you up. When it's time to console, there's no one to catch you when you're feeling hollow inside. I've stared at the ceiling at night, running through the choices I've made—did I handle that right? Should I have been stricter? Softer? You become both the nurturer and the enforcer, juggling the delicate dance of love and discipline, while quietly questioning if you're striking the right balance.

Time becomes something you stretch and twist until it almost breaks. There's never enough of it. You cut into your sleep to finish work projects or fold laundry. You miss reading a book or simply sitting in silence, because the demands never pause. Self-care slips through the cracks. My nails go unpainted, my hair longer between cuts, and my wardrobe the same as it was two years ago. It's the small things that get sacrificed on the altar of necessity, but the loss accumulates. I've gone weeks without a moment to breathe deeply, to think about myself beyond the role of mother, employee, and caregiver.

The isolation? It's palpable. The quiet when the kids are finally asleep, the evenings where you feel the weight of everyone else's life moving on—friends with partners, family gatherings where you're the odd one out. And dating? It's not just finding someone for you; it's about finding someone safe, kind, and stable—someone who won't unravel the fragile structure you've built for your children. I've canceled dates last minute because a babysitter fell through, or because deep down, I wasn't ready to bring someone new into the sacred, hard-earned space I've created for my kids.

Yet amid the storm of responsibilities, there's a lifeline. For me, that lifeline has been faith. It's in those moments when I feel utterly alone, overwhelmed by all that I can't control, that I've felt a whisper—something larger than me, a steady presence in the chaos. Faith, to me, is more than belief; it's a daily practice. It's found in whispered prayers as I drive the kids to school, in the moments before I drift to sleep, asking for the strength to get up and do it all again tomorrow. It's in the community of others who share my values, offer meals when money is tight, or simply sit with me when the weight feels unbearable. Faith doesn't solve everything, but it stitches me back together when I feel frayed, reminding me that I'm not truly alone.

And somehow, through it all, we keep going. Single mothers are the quiet architects of their children's futures. We learn to be both soft and unbreakable, creating a world of love and discipline, even as we face what often feels like a world working against us. We master the art of efficiency, squeezing more into an hour than should be humanly possible, crafting solutions from impossibilities.

But there are moments of grace, too. The smiles, the unprompted hugs, the laughter over dinner, the pride when your child accomplishes something, knowing they've seen you struggle and persevere. These moments remind you that while this journey is harder than ever, it's also richer than you could have anticipated. I've found joy in watching my children grow into resilient, compassionate human beings, knowing they've seen me navigate life's hardest moments with love and determination.

Single motherhood teaches you to embrace imperfection. There are no perfect days, no flawless routines, but that's the beauty of it. You learn to find victory in the small things—in the bedtime story you read, the quiet conversation you had with your teenager after a tough day. You learn that your best, even when it feels insufficient, is more than enough.

And perhaps, the greatest gift single motherhood offers is this: it teaches you to forgive yourself. To let go of the constant pressure to be everything to everyone, and to show your children what it means to be human. That love, persistence, and showing up, even on the hardest days, are what truly matter.

This journey isn't for the faint of heart. But during the chaos, the fatigue, and the doubts, we discover a kind of strength we never knew existed. And with it, the profound beauty that comes from love forged in the fires of adversity.

Chapter 1

ANCHORED IN FAITH – A SINGLE MOTHER'S SPIRITUAL JOURNEY

I never knew how strong I was until I became a single mom,
and being strong was the only choice I had.
— Proud Happy Mama

On a quiet morning, I sit by the kitchen table, a mug of coffee cooling in my hands. Through the window, the early light spills across the floor, catching on the clutter of the morning rush—a lone sneaker under a chair, cereal bowls scattered like remnants of a small battlefield, a crayon drawing taped crookedly to the wall. The house is momentarily still, my three children off to school, and for the first time today, I exhale.

In the silence, I feel it: a deep, calm presence, like something larger than myself wrapping around me. The peace is fleeting—soon, I'll dive back into the chaos of work calls, bills, and laundry—but this small moment is mine. I close my eyes and breathe in and out, letting a quiet prayer form without words. This, I realize, is how faith has taken root in my life. Not in grand gestures or even regular Sunday church visits (though I try), but here, in the creases of my days, in these stolen minutes where I can remember that I am not alone.

Growing up, faith was ritual, routine. My family's church was a bright building with stained glass windows and familiar songs, a place where we gathered each Sunday, clean and smiling. Faith felt like something you wore, like your Sunday best—put on for special occasions, then carefully folded away. But now, in the hard light of single motherhood, faith has become something raw and vital, woven into the fabric of everyday survival. I don't have the luxury of folding it away. I need it as much as I need food, as much as I need sleep.

The Pillars of My Faith Journey

1. The Power of Prayer and Meditation

At first, prayer felt like an afterthought, something I would squeeze in after everyone was finally asleep. I muttered a few lines under my breath before I collapsed into bed. But over time, prayer became a thread I could pull at any moment, anchoring me to something steady. I'd whisper thanks while scrubbing pots and beg for patience as my toddler flung another plate of food to the floor. When exhaustion fogged my brain, I'd take a breath and say, "God, give me strength." It wasn't eloquent, but it was real. And each time, a small sense of relief would settle over me, as if someone had placed a gentle hand on my shoulder, saying, "You're not alone."

Meditation came later, almost by accident. One night, after an especially long day, I sat cross-legged on the floor, closed my eyes, and focused on breathing. In the stillness, I let myself imagine God's presence surrounding me, warm and steady. For those few minutes, the weight of the world lifted. I realized I didn't need a formal ritual or sacred space—only a willingness to sit, listen, and let myself be held.

2. Scripture as a Guide and Comfort

The Bible had always been there, of course, but now its words began to speak to me in a way they never had before. I remember stumbling across a verse in the early hours of a sleepless night: *"My grace is sufficient for you, for my power is made perfect in weakness"* (2 Corinthians 12:9). I read it again and again, letting it sink in. Here I was, feeling weak, stretched thin; sure I was failing in a dozen ways—and here was a reminder that my weakness wasn't something to hide or overcome. It was a doorway, a place where God could enter, filling the gaps I couldn't bridge alone.

When the weight of everything felt too much, I'd return to that verse, holding it close like a talisman. "In my weakness, there is strength," I'd murmur, hoping the words would seep into my bones, reminding me that it was okay to falter. I didn't have to carry it all by myself.

3. Living My Faith

True faith, I learned, wasn't just something you practice in a church pew. It's in the everyday choices, the small acts of patience, kindness, forgiveness. I tried to show this to my kids in small ways—letting the car that cut me off merge in front of us without a curse, choosing calm words when I felt like yelling, reminding them (and myself) that we could be the love we hoped to find in the world.

One day, my eldest came to me after a rough day at school. "Mom, can we pray about it?" he asked, his small face serious. I took his hands in mine, grateful that he saw our faith as something real and useful, not a chore, but a source of comfort. At that moment, he was learning something that would last longer than any lecture or punishment.

4. Finding Mentors and Community

When I finally joined a Bible study group for single mothers, I was nervous. I worried I'd be judged, that my doubts and struggles would seem petty, or that I'd find only superficial platitudes. Instead, I found women like me, who knew the exact texture of exhaustion and the strange mix of pride and guilt that comes from doing it all on your own. We shared laughter, tears, advice—and sometimes just a sympathetic silence, which was a balm all its own. These women became my sisters in spirit, a network of understanding that I didn't realize I'd been longing for.

5. Cultivating Gratitude

Amidst the chaos, I began a small ritual: each night, after the kids were asleep, I'd jot down three things I was grateful for. Some days, it was hard to find even one, but I'd push myself—a good cup of coffee, a neighbor who watched the kids for an hour, a moment of laughter over dinner. Slowly, this habit shifted something in me. I began to see that even in the mess, there were gifts. I wasn't just getting through; I was being given glimpses of grace in the smallest moments.

With time, I began to notice how my deepening faith touched every part of my life:

Emotional Support: When I felt hollowed out by loneliness or worry, faith became my quiet companion, a reminder that I was deeply loved and never, ever alone.

Decision-Making: From choosing a new school to deciding whether to work overtime, I learned to turn inward first, asking for guidance in prayer. It seemed like placing each decision in a trusted hand, waiting for a small nudge in the right direction.

Purpose and Meaning: I stopped seeing myself as just "getting by." Instead, I felt called to something greater—to raise children who knew love, kindness, and resilience. Single motherhood wasn't just my struggle, it was my mission.

Resilience: Faith reminded me that I could rise again, no matter how many times life knocked me down. With God beside me, I could face anything—the unexpected bills, the sickness, the relentless schedule—and still find strength for tomorrow.

Teaching Faith to My Children

As my faith deepened, I saw my children begin to mirror it in their own ways. We'd pray together before meals or before a big test, and they'd ask questions that made me smile, made me proud. Faith was no longer something I had to "teach" them. It was something we lived, breathed, and discovered together.

In this journey of single motherhood, faith has been my steady ground, my quiet strength. It hasn't solved every problem, nor removed every obstacle, but it has transformed me—made me gentler, stronger, and braver. And it's this foundation, this unbreakable connection, that I carry forward into the chapters ahead, knowing that whatever comes, I do not

face it alone.

Chapter 2

CONQUERING MOUNTAINS – THE PHYSICAL CHALLENGES OF SINGLE MOTHERHOOD

It's not the mountain we conquer, but ourselves.
-Edmund Hilary

I feel it in my bones first—the ache that settles deep, whispering reminders of all the bags I've carried, all the nights I've held my children close through fevers, and all the floors scrubbed at the end of a long day. My muscles carry the quiet stories of single motherhood: the endless lifting, the perpetual movement, the quiet strength it takes to keep a household running on the fuel of sheer determination. I'm tired, but the kind of tired that teaches you your own resilience. Every step feels like climbing, but here's the thing about mountains: they make you stronger, even as they take every last ounce of what you've got.

When I became a single mother, I didn't know how physical the journey would be. I expected sleepless nights and never-ending laundry. But I hadn't realized how raising children alone would make my body a battlefield, a place where exhaustion and resilience collide each day. There's a different kind of tiredness in doing it all on your own, a weight that sinks deeper than muscles and bones. It's an ache of body and spirit, one that doesn't ask if you're ready, only if you're willing to keep going.

The Everyday Mountains We Climb

It starts with the small things—the baby carrier digging into my shoulders, the groceries piled high in both hands while a toddler dangles off my hip, the car seat that never seems to buckle without a fight. My hands grow calloused from gripping too many things at once, and my back protests at night from bending, lifting, carrying. I learned to move in efficient sweeps, shoulders braced, legs steady, always ready to catch, comfort, or clean up.

And then, there are the invisible weights. The tension knots itself into the back of my neck as I lie awake, worrying over bills or replaying a hard conversation with my teenager. The headaches that creep in after a day of juggling work deadlines and spelling tests. The exhaustion that drifts over me like fog after days of managing sick kids, when sleep is a luxury I can't afford.

One night stands out in my memory. My youngest was burning with fever, and I spent hours by her bedside, drifting in and out of fitful sleep in an armchair pulled up close. Every so often, I'd check her temperature, stroke her hair, and whisper reassurances in the dark. By morning, I felt like a hollow shell, running on nothing but love and worry. My body was heavy, every limb aching, but the day was just beginning. I had other children to feed, work to complete, and a household to maintain. There was no option to pause. I simply had to stand up, stretch out the stiffness, and start again.

In these moments, I learned that single motherhood is an exercise in physical endurance. You don't get a partner to take over when you're spent; there's no tag team waiting to step in. You keep moving because there's no alternative, and somehow, you find strength in places you didn't know existed.

The Balancing Act: Self-Care in a Selfless Role

In the blur of caregiving, self-care feels like a distant memory. I've skipped meals because feeding everyone else came first. I've let exercise slide, convinced that chasing toddlers and hauling groceries would have to count as my workout. Doctor's appointments for myself were ignored, put off until some unknown "later" when things would get easier.

One day, I caught sight of myself in the mirror—tired eyes, shoulders slumped, a reflection that seemed foreign. I couldn't remember the last time I checked in on my health, and it hit me like a wave: in pouring everything I had into my children, I was leaving nothing for myself. And yet, how could I expect to care for them if I ran myself into the ground?

It was a hard truth to swallow, but an important one: self-care isn't selfish. It's survival. If I wanted to be strong enough to continue climbing these mountains, I had to start treating my own well-being as precious, not expendable.

Illness and Injury: When the World Doesn't Stop

I remember the first time I got seriously ill as a single mother—a fever so high I could barely see straight, aches in every joint, exhaustion so deep it felt like drowning. I lay in bed, listening to my children moving through the house, needing me, the day-to-day routines still ticking away even as my body screamed for rest. There was no pause button, no one to step in while I recovered. I had to get up, fever and all, and tend to my family.

Somehow, I got through it. But it was a humbling experience, one that forced me to reach out. I called friends asking if they could help with childcare. I leaned on family for meals and favors, swallowing my pride in favor of survival. It was a lesson I had to learn the hard way: asking for help isn't a weakness, it's courage. It's acknowledging that I am human, that sometimes I need a hand to hold, someone to share the weight.

The Mental-Physical Connection: When the Mind Wears Out the Body

The stress of single parenting isn't just emotional; it etches itself into the body. I carry my worries in clenched shoulders and tense muscles, my anxieties swirling into headaches and stomach pains. When the mind is heavy, the body follows. And when the body falters, my patience thins, my resilience cracks, and everything feels harder.

I began to see that caring for my physical health wasn't just about avoiding illness. It was about preserving my mental strength, and the resilience I needed to be the mother my children deserved. I started paying attention to the signals—when my body asked for rest, when my mind needed a break when I was stretching myself too thin. It was a slow process, learning to listen to myself as closely as I listened to my children. But gradually, I learned to honor the limits I had once ignored

Letting Go of the Superwoman Myth

There's a pressure that comes with single motherhood, an invisible expectation to be Superwoman—to handle it all with grace, to keep the house spotless, to excel in work, to be endlessly patient and present. I've pushed myself to the brink so many times, trying to live up to an impossible standard. I'd look around at the toys on the floor, the dishes in the sink, and hear a voice whispering, *"You're not doing enough"*. *You're supposed to be better than this.*

But over time, I've learned that "Superwoman" is a myth, a weight that no one should carry. There's strength in admitting when I'm struggling, and resilience in allowing myself to be imperfect. My children don't need a superhero; they need a human mother, who rests when she's tired, and who knows how to forgive herself for the days that aren't perfect.

Strategies for Survival: Building Physical Resilience

With time, I've developed small routines, and ways to preserve my physical health without sacrificing the care I give my children. Here's what has helped me stay strong in body and mind.

1. Prioritizing Sleep: I treat sleep as non-negotiable. Dishes can wait, emails can wait—sleep cannot. I am a better mother, a better everything when I am rested.

2. Moving with Intention: Exercise has become something I incorporate naturally into my day. I dance with my kids in the kitchen, do squats as I fold laundry, or take walks with the stroller. Every bit counts.

3. Fueling My Body: I've stopped seeing food as a convenience and started seeing it as fuel. I keep quick, healthy snacks around, things I can grab on the go to avoid the crash that comes from living off coffee alone.

4. Teachable Moments: My children help with simple chores, not just because it lightens my load, but also because it teaches them responsibility. It's a small way to show them that a family is a team, a shared effort.

5. Mindfulness and Stress Relief: I practice deep breathing, even if it's just a few minutes while waiting for water to boil. A few breaths, a moment of calm—it makes a difference in how I face the rest of the day.

6. Ergonomic Adjustments: I've made small changes, like switching to a backpack for diaper bags or adjusting my work desk, to protect my body from unnecessary strain.

7. Reaching Out: Building a village—a network of friends, family, and other single parents—has been my greatest survival tool. There's no shame in asking for help, and I've found strength in the support others are willing to give.

Reframing Success: The Path to Self-Compassion

Ultimately, I've redefined what success looks like as a single mother. It's not about perfection, endless energy, or keeping up appearances. It's about showing up, even on the days when I feel empty. It's about small victories—the mornings we get out the door on time, the dinners shared at a messy table, the laughter that breaks through the exhaustion. It's about recognizing that every step forward, no matter how small, is an act of courage.

The mountains I climb are real, but they have given me a strength I never knew I had. I'm learning, one day at a time, that I don't have to be invincible. I just have to be present. I just have to keep going. And in that persistence, in the love and care I pour into my children and myself, I am already enough.

Chapter 3
NAVIGATING FINANCIAL HARDSHIP

Wealth consists not in having great possessions, but in having few wants. — Epictetus

Every week, I sit at the kitchen table, pen in hand, calculator poised, receipts spread out before me like puzzle pieces that never quite fit. Each dollar has a purpose—rent, food, school supplies, bills—and there's rarely anything left to cushion the fall when life inevitably throws another unexpected expense my way. This balancing act has become my ritual, a dance of numbers and necessity, a constant reminder of the narrow line I walk between stability and struggle. It's exhausting, humbling, and sometimes deeply isolating. Yet, navigating financial hardship has also taught me resilience, resourcefulness, and a kind of quiet pride in doing what it takes to keep my family afloat.

Overcoming Stigma

There was a day, early in my journey as a single mother, when I found myself standing in line at the grocery store, a stack of food stamps in my hand, heart pounding as if the clerk and every shopper behind me could see every worry, every late-night struggle. I held my head high, but inside, I felt a pang of shame—a whispering voice that asked if I'd somehow failed. I'd grown up hearing words about self-sufficiency and pride, and here I was, depending on assistance to feed my children.

But over time, that shame began to dissolve. I realized these programs existed for a reason—that asking for help didn't make me any less capable, any less strong. It took courage to stand in that line, to set aside pride in favor of my children's well-being. Food stamps, like every other form of support, were tools, not crutches. They allowed me to provide for my family in difficult times, and put nutritious meals on the table without sacrificing rent or utility payments. Accepting help didn't mean I had failed; it meant I was doing everything in my power to care for my kids.

I came to see the stigma as society's judgment, not my own truth. The people who whisper about "handouts" and "welfare queens" have never faced the relentless pressure of single parenthood or felt the tightness in their chest when choosing between food and heat. Overcoming that stigma meant reshaping my own perspective—recognizing that the greatest strength sometimes lies in knowing when to lean on others.

Seeking Resources and Support

Navigating financial hardship is not just about making do with less. It's about becoming a hunter-gatherer of resources and finding creative ways to fill the gaps. In those early days, I learned to use every form of support I could find. Community food banks became familiar stops, offering bags of staples that would stretch my grocery budget. Non-profits provided help with school supplies and holiday gifts, sparing me the heartache of explaining to my kids why Santa might not visit this year.

I joined support groups for single parents, both in person and online. These groups weren't just places to vent—they became networks of shared knowledge, places where I could learn about grants, assistance programs, and budgeting tips from others living through the same struggles. There's a unique comfort in knowing you're not alone, that someone else understands the daily juggling act of bills and paychecks. We became each other's lifeline, pooled resources, shared advice, and sometimes even babysat in exchange for groceries or other favors.

Church and faith-based organizations provided not only financial assistance but also a sense of community. The warmth of a homemade casserole dropped off by a parishioner, the anonymous envelope with a gift card left in my mailbox—these gestures reminded me that there was kindness in the world, that I was part of something bigger than myself.

Budgeting and Financial Management

There's a level of precision that comes with budgeting as a single parent. Every dollar is measured, and every expense evaluated. In my world, there's no such thing as impulse buying; there's no room for "extras." I've learned to sit down each month and create a strict budget, allocate funds to essentials—rent, utilities, groceries—and adjust as needed when something unexpected comes up. Coupons, discounts, and bulk buying have become essential tools in my arsenal. I find satisfaction in squeezing the most out of each dollar, knowing that every bit of savings makes a difference.

Teaching my children about money has become part of this journey. I show them the value of each dollar, let them compare prices in the grocery store, and explain why we can't buy everything they want. It's not always easy to have those conversations, but I know that these lessons will serve them well. They're learning resilience, learning to appreciate what they have, and learning material possessions don't measure abundance alone.

Saving in the Face of Scarcity

There's a line item in my budget labeled "savings," but most months, it sits untouched. For a long time, the idea of setting aside money felt impossible—how could I save when I could barely make ends meet? But I began to realize that even a small cushion, even a few dollars here and there, could be a lifesaver in an emergency.

I started with tiny steps—automating five dollars to a savings account each month, setting aside any loose change, and selling old clothes or unused items for a few extra dollars. Little by little, those small efforts added up. It was slow, but it gave me a sense of security, a small buffer between us and the next unexpected crisis.

Some months, I had to dip into that savings just to cover an urgent bill or a doctor's visit, but I didn't let that discourage me. I kept adding to it, bit by bit. For the first time, I felt like I was building something for the future, no matter how modest. This small act of saving became a quiet act of defiance, a way of saying, "I will be okay. We will be okay."

Balancing Immediate Needs with Long-term Goals

One of the hardest aspects of single parenthood is balancing the immediate needs—food, shelter, clothing—with the long-term dreams I hold for myself and my children. There are times when every dollar I earn goes toward keeping the lights on or putting dinner on the table, and the future feels distant and out of reach. Yet I know that for my children's sake, I have to keep looking forward, even when it's difficult to see beyond the present.

I try to find ways to invest in myself, even if it's just taking a free online class or reading a book on career advancement borrowed from the library. I want my children to see that I am working toward something bigger—that we are not just surviving, but slowly, steadily, building a life. Every small step I take towards self-improvement is a step towards a future where financial hardship won't define us.

Dealing with Unexpected Expenses

If there's one certainty in life, it's that the unexpected will happen. The car will break down. A child will get sick. An appliance will decide to stop working just as winter begins. As a single parent, these moments hit hard. With no backup income or second paycheck, each unexpected cost feels like a landslide, threatening to bury us under its weight.

I've learned to prepare as best as possible, building an emergency fund slowly, learning basic repairs, and calling in favors when I need to. I've become resourceful, finding ways to patch things up, stretch the budget, and make do with what we have. And when the burden feels too heavy, I lean on the community I've built—friends, family, and church members who understand that no one gets through life alone.

The Role of Faith in Financial Struggles

Through all this, my faith has been a constant. When the numbers don't add up, when the bills pile high, when the worry settles like a weight on my chest, I turn to prayer. My conversations with God aren't grand or poetic—they're simple and raw. "Help me through this. Give me strength. Show me the way." My faith has become a source of resilience, a reminder that I am never truly alone in this journey.

My faith community has been a lifeline, offering practical support when I need it most. There are times when I can't see a way forward, but through prayer and reflection, I find the courage to keep going. Faith doesn't erase the hardship, but it gives me the strength to bear it, and the hope to believe in something better.

Teaching Children About Financial Realities

In a world that values material wealth, teaching my children about the realities of our situation has been both a challenge and an opportunity. I want them to feel safe, know they are loved and provided for, but I also want them to understand the value of money, to appreciate what we have, rather than longing for what we don't.

I talk to them about budgeting, saving, and making choices. When they ask for something out of reach, I explain why in a way they can understand. I involve my older children in simple decisions, letting them see how we prioritize, and how we make the most of what we have. They're learning resilience, learning to find joy in simple things, and learning that true wealth isn't just about possessions.

Seeking Additional Income Sources

To give us more breathing room, I've explored every possible avenue for earning extra income. I've taken on freelance work, picked up weekend shifts, even sold handmade crafts online. Each side gig adds a little more security, including a little more stability. It's not always sustainable—I have to balance work with time for my children, with rest, and my limits—but every effort brings us closer to the life I want for us.

Maintaining a Positive Outlook

Despite the struggles, I choose to celebrate the small victories. A week with all bills paid on time. A family meal where we laugh instead of worry. A dollar saved, a moment of peace, a day without stress. These are the things that sustain me, the quiet joys that remind me of what truly matters.

At the end of each day, I remind myself that wealth isn't just what's in my bank account. It's the love I share with my children, the resilience we build together, the gratitude we feel for the roof over our heads, and the food on our table. I may not have much, but I have what matters, and that knowledge keeps me grounded.

Navigating financial hardship as a single parent is a journey of resilience, learning to ask for help, and finding pride in small victories. It's not easy, and it's not without sacrifice, but each challenge shapes me, strengthens me, and shows my children the true meaning of perseverance. We may not have much by the world's standards, but we are rich in love, faith, and strength we find together. That, I tell myself every day, is enough.

CHAPTER 4
RAISING CHILDREN AS A SINGLE PARENT

To be in your children's memories tomorrow, you have to be in their lives today. — Barbara Johnson

Every night, as the house settles into quiet and my children drift off to sleep, I pause and look around at the small world I've built for us—a world where laughter can fill a room as easily as worry, where peanut butter and jelly can feel like a feast, and where love is woven into every corner. Single parenthood is a journey filled with impossible choices and invisible sacrifices, but above all, it is about creating a safe harbor for my children—a place where they feel secure, cherished, and understood.

Creating Stability Amidst the Storm

For single parents, stability is more than just a word; it's a mission, a commitment. My priority has always been the basics: a roof over their heads, warm meals on the table, lights that flicker on when they flip a switch. I've faced countless moments of financial worry, times when I wasn't sure if I'd make it to the end of the month. But I knew, with unwavering certainty, that I would always find a way to provide the essentials for my children. They might not have everything, but they will always have enough.

Yet, stability goes beyond the physical. It's the consistent rhythms we create, the bedtime stories read in whispers, the Saturday morning pancakes, the school drop-offs and pick-ups. These routines become anchors, small but sturdy, offering my children a sense of predictability and normalcy in a world that sometimes feels unsteady.

There was a time when all we had in the pantry was bread, peanut butter, and jelly. We gathered around the kitchen table, spreading our meager ingredients and laughing as we crafted our sandwiches. "Peanut butter and jelly again?" one of them groaned, but a grin followed it, a spark of joy in his eyes. I looked at them, my heart swelling with gratitude, and thought, *Yes, but we ate.* Those words became a quiet mantra—a reminder that even in our simplest moments, we were together, we were enough.

The Dual Role: Balancing Nurture and Discipline

Single parenthood requires a balancing act like no other. I am both the gentle comforter and the firm disciplinarian, the one who tucks them in at night and the one who enforces the rules. There's no second parent to share the weight of these roles, no one to play "good cop" when I'm exhausted from being the "bad cop."

Some days, this dual role feels overwhelming. I worry if I'm being too strict, or if I'm spoiling them in my efforts to make up for what we lack. I remind myself that every decision I make comes from a place of love, even when it's hard, even when they don't understand. Over time, I've learned to trust my instincts, to know that I am giving them what they need: a blend of boundaries and compassion, a mixture of firmness and warmth.

Resilience Through Hardship: Lessons in Gratitude

Single parenthood has taught me—and by extension, my children—that resilience is not just about surviving hard times, but about finding gratitude within them. There's a quiet power in appreciating what we have, even when it feels like it's not enough. I've taught my children to cherish the little things: the warmth of a cozy blanket, the joy of movie nights at home, the laughter we share over silly games that cost nothing but time.

One evening, as we sat around the table eating another humble meal, my daughter looked up at me and said, "Mom, thank you for making dinner." I smiled, taken aback by her words. Here was a child who understood, at such a young age, the value of effort, of love given freely. Moments like these remind me that my children learn not only to survive but also to thrive, and appreciate the blessings woven into our everyday lives.

Building Traditions and Memories

In a home where resources are often limited, I've discovered that the most meaningful memories are created from the simplest moments. We have movie nights with popcorn, where we pile up on the couch under blankets and laugh until our stomachs ache. We take walks to the park, where we play tag or skip stones across the water. These small traditions, repeated over time, become the fabric of our family.

Each tradition, no matter how small, becomes part of their story—a story of love, resilience, and togetherness. It's my way of giving them a childhood filled with joy and comfort, even if I can't give them everything the world might tell them they need.

Navigating Guilt and the Quest for Balance

If there's one emotion that haunts every parent, it's guilt. Guilt for not being able to provide more, guilt for time lost to work, guilt for moments when exhaustion gets the better of me. There are nights when I lie awake, replay the day, and question whether I could have done more or been better.

But over time, I've come to realize that quality matters far more than quantity. A few moments of true presence—listening to their stories, laughing at their jokes, holding them when they're sad—mean more than hours spent together without connection. My children need me to be engaged and loving, not perfect. They need me to show up with an open heart, to make the most of the time we have, and to forgive myself for the moments when I fall short.

The Power of Communication

Open, honest communication has become a cornerstone of our family. I believe in speaking openly to my children about our circumstances in ways they can understand. They know we're a team, that each of us has a role to play in making our family work. I've found that sharing some challenges—not in a way that burdens them, but in a way that includes them—creates a bond of trust and mutual respect.

When there's a tough month, I explain why we need to be careful with money. When I'm tired, I let them know that I'm human, that I'm doing my best, but sometimes need a little grace too. They're learning that family is about supporting one another, that love is a partnership, not just something they receive passively.

Providing Positive Role Models

As a single mother, I'm acutely aware of the importance of role models. I want my children to see examples of kindness, integrity, and resilience from people of all backgrounds and genders. I introduce them to mentors, friends, and family members who inspire them, plus show them different ways to be strong and compassionate.

We talk about family in broader terms—how families come in all shapes and sizes, and how love doesn't always look like the picture-perfect images on TV. I want them to know that their family is whole just as it is. They're learning that family is defined by love and commitment, not by the number of people in the household.

The Joys and Rewards of the Journey

For all the exhaustion, the self-doubt, the long nights, and tight budgets, there are moments of indescribable joy. Watching my children grow, seeing them become resilient, compassionate, and independent—that is the greatest reward. Our journey together is woven with challenges, but it's also filled with laughter, warmth, and an unbreakable bond.

In the quiet moments—when my child slips their hand into mine, or says "I love you" out of the blue—I'm reminded of why I chose this path, why I fight so hard to give them a life filled with love and stability.

The sacrifices fade, and all that remains is the overwhelming gratitude I feel for being their mother.

The Legacy of Love and Resilience

As my children grow, I can see the fruits of our journey together. They are empathetic, understanding, and unafraid of hard work. They know what it means to cherish what they have, face life's challenges with courage, and find beauty in the simplest things. In raising them alone, I've given them not just a home, but a foundation of resilience and strength they can carry forward.

Raising children as a single parent is not about having everything or doing it all perfectly. It's about showing up, day after day, with love and dedication. It's about creating a home where, despite the odds, children feel valued, supported, and deeply loved. I may not be able to give them everything, but I can give them what matters most: a mother who believes in them, who fights for them, and who will always be there, cheering them on every step of the way.

CHAPTER 5
SELF-CARE AND GROWTH

You can't pour from an empty cup. Take care of yourself first.
— Unknown

There's a myth that single parents must be selfless to the point of sacrifice, that every waking moment should be devoted to their children, or every ounce of energy given to keep the family going. It's a myth I bought into for a long time. I believed that if I wasn't constantly tending to my children's needs, I was somehow failing them. But over time, I realized something vital: my children don't need a mother who's always there but running on fumes. They need a mother who's healthy, present, and fulfilled—a mother who shows them what it means to take care of herself as much as she cares for them.

Self-care isn't selfish; it's survival. It's about making sure I'm well enough to keep being the mother they need, day after day. And just as importantly, it's about setting an example. I want my children to grow up knowing that taking care of yourself is essential, and that pursuing your own goals and dreams doesn't detract from your love for your family. Rather, it adds to it. So, this chapter is dedicated to the journey of self-care and personal growth, a journey that has taught me that nurturing myself is ultimately one of the most loving things I can do for my children.

Making Time for Yourself

As a single parent, time feels like the rarest of luxuries. There's always something that needs doing—the dishes piling up, the endless laundry, the emails from teachers, the meals to prepare. Taking even a few minutes to yourself can feel like a guilty indulgence. But I've learned that if I don't take time to recharge, I eventually reach a point where I'm not much use to anyone, least of all my children.

So, I carve out small pockets of time. Sometimes it's waking up a few minutes early to enjoy a quiet cup of coffee in the stillness of the morning. Sometimes it's taking a long bath after the kids are asleep, letting the warmth soak away the stress of the day. These moments may be small, but they're vital. They're a chance to remind myself that I am a person, not just a mother. I'm allowed to take up space, breathe, relax, and reconnect with who I am outside my role as a parent.

Self-care can be as simple as reading a chapter of a book before bed, going for a short walk, or listening to a favorite song. The important part is permitting yourself to do it, to say, "I deserve this." Because you do.

Setting Personal Goals

One of the most transformative decisions I made was to set a personal goal outside of parenting. For so long, my focus was solely on my children and our daily survival. But I started to feel like I was losing a part of myself like my identity was shrinking. I wanted to feel proud of myself for something beyond motherhood, to show my children that it's okay to have dreams and ambitions, even when life feels overwhelming.

So I picked a goal—something small but meaningful. It could be learning a new skill, taking a class, or even something as simple as finishing a book or gathering dust on my shelf. The goal itself wasn't the point; it was the act of choosing something for myself, setting a target, and working towards it.

When I began pursuing my own goals, my children noticed. They asked questions, and watched as I studied, practiced or worked. They saw that their mother had passions, and believed in self-improvement and growth. It was a quiet lesson, but a powerful one. I taught them, without even realizing it, that life is more than just duty and survival. It's also about exploring, learning, and growing—no matter your circumstances.

The Importance of Showing Up for Yourself

In the whirlwind of single parenthood, it's easy to lose sight of your own needs. I know I did for a long time. But I've come to understand that showing up for myself—honoring my own health, my dreams, my happiness—is not only a gift to me, it's a gift to my children. It's my way of showing them that they deserve to show up for themselves, too.

Showing up for myself means going to the doctor when I need to, eating well, getting rest, and not putting off self-care until I reach the point of burnout. It means reminding myself that I am worthy of love and care, not only from others but also from myself. It's about recognizing that I am more than just a provider; I am a whole person with needs that deserve attention.

When I make time for myself, I permit my children to prioritize their well-being as they grow. They see that taking care of yourself isn't an afterthought; it's part of being a responsible, fulfilled person.

Navigating the Guilt of Self-Care

Self-care sounds wonderful in theory, but for single parents, it often comes with a hefty side of guilt. The time I spend on myself should be time I could spend with my children. The money I might put toward my own goals feels like money that could go toward them. Every decision to care for myself feels, at first, like a choice that takes away from them.

But I've learned to reframe that guilt. Self-care isn't something I do *instead* of caring for my children; it's something I do so that I can *keep* caring for them. When I feel guilty about taking time for myself, I remind myself that my children deserve a mother who isn't depleted, who has energy, who can laugh, play and be present. They deserve a mother who is happy, who has passions and goals and feels fulfilled.

Over time, the guilt has softened, replaced by a quiet confidence that caring for myself is part of caring for them. They may not understand it now, but one day, I hope they'll look back and see that I taught them by example—that it's okay to take up space, value yourself, and nourish your own soul.

Modeling Self-Care for Your Children

Children learn so much by watching us. They see how we handle stress, how we take care of ourselves, how we balance work and rest. When I take time for myself, when I set and pursue my own goals, I show my children that self-care is not a luxury, but a necessity.

I want them to grow up knowing that it's okay to say, "I need a break." I want them to know that their dreams matter and that they are allowed to chase their passions, even when life gets busy. By prioritizing my self-care, I'm laying the groundwork for them to feel comfortable doing the same as they grow older. I'm teaching them that a well-lived life is one where you take care of yourself and others.

Celebrating Small Wins

In a life filled with challenges, I've learned to celebrate small victories. Sometimes, self-care doesn't look like a spa day or weekend getaway. Sometimes, it's as simple as making it through a tough day with grace, finding five minutes to meditate, or accomplishing one small goal I set for myself. I take pride in these little achievements because they remind me that I am making progress, that I am growing.

Every small win is a step toward a life where I feel balanced and fulfilled, a life where I am more than just a caregiver. It's a life that feels full and meaningful, not just for my children, but for myself as well.

Rediscovering Your Own Dreams

Self-care isn't just about rest; it's about growth. It's about reconnecting with the parts of myself that existed before I became a parent, rediscovering passions and dreams that might have been set aside. I want my children to know that their mother has dreams and that it's okay to chase them, even if it takes time, even if the journey is slow.

Whether it's writing, learning a new skill, exploring a hobby, or furthering my education, I'm permitting myself to dream again. And in doing so, I'm showing my children that life is a continuous journey of learning and becoming. They see that their mother is more than just a source of support; she is a person with her own aspirations. This, I hope, will give them the courage to pursue their own dreams one day.

In the End, It's About Balance

Self-care and growth are about finding balance: between my role as a mother and my identity as an individual, between the needs of my children and the needs of my own heart. It's not easy, and it's not perfect, but I'm learning that both parts can coexist. I can be a dedicated mother and a fulfilled individual. I can care deeply for my children, while also nurturing my soul.

My children are watching me, learning from me. I want them to see self-care is strength, growth is resilience, and that life is about more than just meeting demands—it's about finding joy, balance, and purpose. In prioritizing my well-being, I am showing them what it means to live a full, authentic life.

In the end, taking care of myself is one of the most loving things I can do for them. It's how I ensure that I can continue to show up as the best version of myself: a version that is not only their mother, but also a person with hopes, dreams, and a heart full of love for herself and for them.

CHAPTER 6
LESSONS LEARNED AND VICTORIES WON

The struggle you're in today is developing the strength you need for tomorrow. — Robert Tew

There's a saying that goes, "You never know what someone is carrying." People see you out in the world—your children dressed in their best, your face pulled into a smile—and they assume everything's in place. But they don't see the empty pantry at home, the negative bank balance you've been ignoring, the nights you lie awake, heart pounding, wondering how you'll make it through another day. They don't see the battles fought in silence; the victories won just by surviving.

Single parenthood has taught me countless lessons, each earned through struggle, each one a quiet victory in its way. I've learned to live on my timeline and resist the pressure of keeping up with anyone else's pace. I've come to understand survival is a kind of strength, and that God's timing is not always mine, but it's always right. As I look back, I see how every hardship, every hard-won lesson, and every moment of grace have shaped me into someone I never imagined I could be.

Lesson One: The Power of Patience and Moving at Your Own Pace

In the beginning, I felt the invisible clock ticking. Society, friends, even family—all of them seemed to carry expectations of where I "should" be, and what I "should" have achieved. There were moments when I felt behind, like everyone else was racing ahead while I was stuck in place just trying to survive the day. But single parenthood has taught me that my journey is my own, and I don't have to measure my progress by anyone else's timeline.

When I began to move at my own pace, a strange peace settled over me. I stopped feeling the need to rush, catch up, or reach some imaginary finish line. I learned to focus on what I could do today, with the resources I had, without the pressure of comparison. Some weeks, simply paying the bills and keeping the kids fed felt like a monumental achievement. And that was okay. I was doing the best I could, and that was enough.

In letting go of others' expectations, I found freedom. I learned to move with grace instead of haste, and to take pride in each small step forward. This journey isn't a race; it's a path uniquely mine. And I'm exactly where I'm meant to be.

Lesson Two: The Strength in Showing Up When You're Struggling

People see us out in the world, and assume they know the story. But they don't see the times I've forced myself out of bed, dressed the kids in their best, and painted a smile on my face even when my heart felt heavy. They don't see the days I've shown up to work or school events with a negative balance in my bank account, feeling like I'm carrying the weight of the world alone.

Showing up on those hard days is its own kind of victory. It's an act of resilience, a quiet defiance against the odds. My children see me showing up, not just when things are easy, but when they're hardest. They see that strength isn't about having it all together—it's about standing up and moving forward, even when the ground feels shaky.

Over time, I've learned to celebrate these victories, even if they go unnoticed by the world. Each time I show up despite the struggles, I teach my children that courage is often silent, the real strength isn't flashy or loud—it's simply doing what needs to be done, with love and determination.

Lesson Three: The Grace of God's Timing

There have been moments when I felt like I was at the end of my rope, desperate for relief, for something to change. And just when I thought I couldn't hold on anymore, help would arrive—a check in the mail, a friend offering to watch the kids, a small but needed blessing that reminded me that I wasn't alone. Over and over, I've been shown that God's timing may not match my own, but it is always, always right.

Faith has taught me to trust that what I need will come when I need it, even if it doesn't come when I want it. I've stopped questioning the "why" and "when" of things, and started trusting that I'm exactly where I'm meant to be. I remind myself that I am seen, that my struggles are noticed, that there is a purpose even in the waiting. Each time I place my trust in God's timing, I find a little more peace, a little more patience, and a little more faith in the journey.

Victory Won: Creating a Home Built on Love, Not Material Wealth

People often assume that stability requires financial abundance, but I've learned that true stability is built on something much deeper. My children may not have the latest gadgets or the fanciest clothes, but they have a home filled with love, laughter, and resilience. They know they are safe, cherished, and valued.

Our home is modest, but it's rich in things that money can't buy. We find joy in small rituals—movie nights with popcorn, dance parties in the living room, and bedtime stories that stretch late into the night. I've learned that possessions don't measure wealth. The memories measure it, by the laughter we share, by the love that fills our home.

Creating a home like this is my quiet victory, one that gives me pride. It's proof that I'm giving my children something lasting, meaningful—a foundation of love that will carry them far beyond material comforts.

Victory Two: Teaching My Children Resilience and Gratitude

Through all the ups and downs, my children learn what it means to persevere, be grateful for what they have, and find beauty in simplicity. They're learning that life isn't always easy, but it's always worth showing up for. They see that we may not have everything we want, but we have everything we need.

This lesson is a gift I'm proud to give them. They're growing up knowing that resilience is a strength. The gratitude isn't reserved for abundance but for every moment of love, warmth, and togetherness. They understand that even in hard times, there is something to be thankful for.

Watching them develop these qualities has been one of my greatest victories. They may not have every luxury, but they have something far more valuable: a sense of inner strength, a heart filled with gratitude, and the knowledge that they are loved deeply.

Victory Three: Discovering My Own Inner Strength

If someone had told me years ago what I would face, I wouldn't have believed I could handle it. But each challenge has revealed a strength I never knew I had. I've faced moments of doubt, despair, and fear, and yet I'm still here, still standing, still moving forward.

Single parenthood has shown me that I am capable of more than I ever imagined. I've learned to trust myself, to believe in my resilience, to know that no matter the outcome, I can find a way through. These victories are one of my greatest achievements: the understanding that I am stronger than my circumstances. Everything I need will be provided.

Victory Four: Choosing Faith Over Fear

In the hardest moments, when fear threatens to overwhelm me, I've learned to choose faith. Faith that there is a purpose to my journey, that I am not walking this path alone. In fact, there is a reason for each struggle. So, faith carried me through the darkest nights, reminding me that there is always hope, always light, even when I can't see it.

Choosing faith over fear has been one of the most transformative decisions I've made. It's allowed me to face each day with courage, to believe that every hardship has a purpose, and to trust that I am exactly where I need to be. This faith isn't just a belief; it's a daily choice. A commitment to trust that God's plan for me is greater than my understanding.

Celebrating the Journey

As I look back on the lessons learned and victories won, I see a journey defined by resilience, love, and unwavering faith. There were days I thought I wouldn't make it, moments when the burden felt too heavy, when the loneliness seemed endless. But each step forward, no matter how small, was a victory. Each lesson, no matter how hard-won, became a building block for the person I am today.

In the end, this journey isn't just about surviving, it's about growing, learning, and finding joy amid struggle. It's about showing my children that life may not be easy, but it's beautiful, and every challenge we face makes us stronger.

I may not have riches or luxury, but I have victories that can't be measured in dollars: a home built on love, children raised with resilience and gratitude, and a heart that has learned to trust in God's timing. These are the riches I carry, the treasures I hold close, the proof that every hardship, every lesson, was worth it.

To all those walking a similar path, remember: you're exactly where you're meant to be. Trust in the journey, celebrate each victory and know that you are stronger than you realize. The world may not see your struggles, but each step forward is

a triumph, each lesson a gift. Keep going, keep believing, and
hold close to the faith that has carried you this far. The best is
yet to come.

CHAPTER 7
ENCOURAGEMENT FOR OTHER SINGLE MOTHERS

You may have to fight a battle more than once to win it.
—Margaret Thatcher

To every mother reading this, I want you to know one thing above all else: you are not alone. There are days, I know when it feels like the weight of the world rests squarely on your shoulders. There are nights when the silence is deafening, when the quiet ache of loneliness sits beside you, heavy and unyielding. You may wonder if anyone sees you, if anyone truly understands the depth of your struggles, your fears, your relentless determination to keep going. But you are not alone. There is a sisterhood of single mothers, women who understand, women who are walking similar paths, and most importantly, a God who sees you in every single moment.

Being a single mother is not just a role; it's a journey that demands strength, resilience, and courage, often in the face of overwhelming odds. It's a journey that sometimes feels thankless and exhausting but also filled with purpose, beauty, and grace. You may not feel it every day, but you are doing an extraordinary thing. And as you navigate this path, take heart and remember these words of encouragement.

One Day at a Time

When you look too far ahead, the road can seem impossible. The worries pile up—the bills, appointments, the relentless to-do list. It's easy to feel overwhelmed when you're carrying so much on your own. But here's what I've learned: you don't have to conquer the whole journey at once. Take it one day at a time, and sometimes, one hour or even one minute at a time.

In moments of overwhelm, remind yourself that today is enough. Focus on what you can accomplish right now. You don't have to solve every problem this instant. Sometimes, victory is simply getting through the day, finding small moments of peace, and knowing that tomorrow is a new beginning. Permit yourself to move slowly, breathe, and trust that each step forward—no matter how small—is progress.

Lean on God's Strength

In my hardest moments, when I felt empty and unable to keep going, I found strength in my faith. I learned to depend on God, not just when things were good, but especially when life felt unbearable. There is a unique grace that comes from surrendering your struggles, worries, fears, and trusting that you don't have to bear them alone.

When the weight feels too heavy, turn to God in prayer. Whisper your worries, your doubts, your exhaustion, and ask for the strength to keep going. Faith doesn't erase the challenges, but it gives you the resilience to face them. It reminds you that this journey has a purpose, even if you can't see it yet. Rely on God not just as a last resort, but as your steady foundation, as the one who walks with you every step of the way.

Find a Support System—No Matter How Small

Single motherhood can be isolating, but you don't have to do this alone. Whether it's family, friends, or a community group, having someone to lean on can make all the difference. Even if it's just one person you can call when you're overwhelmed, one friend who understands your struggles, one family member who offers a helping hand—that support can be a lifeline.

If you don't have a family nearby, consider joining a support group for single parents, either locally or online. In these spaces, you'll find other women who understand what you're going through and can share advice, encouragement, or just a listening ear. Being surrounded by people who "get it" can lift some loneliness and remind you that you are part of a larger community, one that supports and uplifts each other.

Celebrate Small Victories

Life as a single mother is often about the small wins—the bills paid on time, a peaceful bedtime, a home-cooked meal after a long day. These moments may feel insignificant, but they are victories, each one proof that you're doing an incredible job. Don't wait for monumental achievements to feel proud of yourself. Every day you get up, show up, and give your best is a day worth celebrating.

When you reach the end of a tough day, take a moment to acknowledge what you accomplished, even if it's just keeping everyone fed and safe. Write down these small victories if it helps. Look back on them in moments of doubt, and remind yourself of your strength. You are doing so much more than you give yourself credit for.

Give Yourself Grace

Perfection is a myth, and trying to live up to an impossible standard only leads to burnout. There will be days when things don't go as planned, when patience wears thin, when exhaustion catches up with you. And that's okay. Give yourself grace to be imperfect, to make mistakes, and have moments when you fall short of your expectations.

Self-compassion is not a luxury; it's a necessity. Treat yourself with the same kindness and understanding you would offer a friend. Remember that you're doing the best you can with what you have, and that's all anyone can ask of you. Embrace your humanity, your imperfections, and trust that your love is more than enough for your children.

Remember That Your Children See Your Strength

You might experience moments where you wonder whether your children recognize the efforts sacrificed or the depth of your love. But rest assured: they notice. They observe your daily presence, the protection you offer, the care and encouragement you provide. While they may not fully grasp every challenge, they instinctively feel the safety, love, and stability you create for them.

Believe me, children are constantly watching and learning from their parents. They see a who perseveres, confronts challenges with bravery, draws strength from faith, and remains resilient during difficult times. Someday, they will reflect on their childhood and realize the magnitude of your dedication. They will feel grateful. You are their role model, their pillar of strength, and a living example of love in action.

Trust in God's Timing

When life feels relentless, when every step forward seems met with two steps back, it's easy to feel discouraged. But trust that there is a purpose to every challenge, a plan that may not be visible yet. God's timing is not always our timing, and sometimes we're called to wait, trust, and keep moving, even when we don't see the outcome.

Faith teaches us patience, and patience teaches us resilience. When the path feels long, lean into your faith. Trust that everything you're going through has a reason, that there is beauty and growth in the struggle, and that one day, the pieces will fall into place. God is with you in every step, guiding you, holding you up, and leading you to exactly where you need to be.

Know That You Are Enough

In a world that constantly tells us we're not doing enough, not giving enough, not *enough* in every possible way, I want you to hear this loud and clear: *You are enough.* Your love, your effort, your presence—these are the things that matter most to your children, not the things you wish you could give them or the moments you think you've fallen short.

You are enough just as you are, in all your struggles, your strengths, your imperfections. Your children are not missing out; they are growing up with a mother who is teaching them resilience, compassion, and the power of love. Trust that what you're giving them is more than enough. They don't need perfection; they need you, exactly as you are.

A Message to Carry Forward

To every mother reading this, remember that your journey is unique, and your strength is unmatched. There will be hard days, days when you wonder if you're doing enough, days when you feel stretched beyond your limits. But know this: you are part of a legacy of strong women, of mothers who have walked this path before, and mothers who walk beside you now.

Every day, you are building a life for your children, creating a foundation of love and resilience that will carry them forward. Take pride in that. Take pride in the fact that you are showing them what it means to keep going, hold faith close, and believe in yourself even when the world feels heavy.

When you feel alone, remember that you're surrounded by a community of women who understand, support you, and cheer you on. And remember, too, that God is with you, guiding each step, lifting you up when you stumble, and offering you strength when yours runs low.

Take it one day at a time. Trust in the journey, lean on your faith, and know, deep in your heart, that you are enough.

You are doing something extraordinary. You are raising a family. And you are not alone.

FINAL THOUGHTS
A JOURNEY OF STRENGTH AND LOVE

Faith is taking the first step even when you don't see the whole staircase. — Martin Luther King Jr.

As I close this book, I want to thank you—whether you're a single mother, a supporter of someone on this journey, or simply someone looking for hope and resilience. Thank you for reading, sharing in my story, and walking this path with me, even for a short while. My name is Latoya Glover, and this book represents not just my journey as a single mother, but also the lessons, the love, and the faith that have carried me through.

When I started this journey, I didn't know what I was capable of. I didn't know how many times I'd have to start over, how many nights I'd lie awake wondering if I was enough, or how many mountains I'd climb without any idea of what lay on the other side. But each day, I took that first step, even when I couldn't see the whole staircase. Step by step, I moved forward, trusting that God would meet me on the journey and somehow find a way.

Being a single mother has been the hardest and most rewarding role I've ever known. It has taught me strength in the face of adversity, patience when life felt impossible, and resilience even when the weight felt unbearable. It has shown me the power of love, the importance of faith, and the beauty in small, everyday victories.

To Every Single Mother Reading This

If there's one thing, I want you to remember, it's this: your struggles do not define you, your past, or the hardships you face. The love defines you as you pour it into your children, as well as the quiet strength you summon each morning, and the faith you carry when the world feels uncertain. You are a testament to resilience, a symbol of grace, and a reflection of the endless power of a mother's love.

Our journeys may look different, but we share a sisterhood of understanding. You're never truly alone in this. Each time you choose to keep going, to put one foot in front of the other, you are part of a legacy of strong women who have carried the weight of the world on their shoulders and still found a way to rise. You are enough just as you are.

Moving Forward with Faith and Purpose

For me, faith has been my anchor, the quiet, steady presence that has grounded me in the midst of every storm. I've learned that I don't have to have all the answers or control every outcome. I just need to trust the journey and take it one step at a time. I've learned that God's timing is perfect, even when it doesn't align with my own. Each moment of grace, each blessing that arrives just when I need it, reminds me that I am seen, loved, and supported.

As I look ahead, I know that challenges will still come. But I also know that I've built something strong within myself, within my family, and within my faith. I know that I can face whatever comes next, because I've seen what I'm capable of, and I trust the One who walks beside me.

A Message for My Children

To my beautiful children, if you ever read this, I want you to know how deeply you are loved. Everything I've done, every sacrifice, every sleepless night, every decision, was made with you in mind. You are my greatest blessing, my heart, my reason for persevering even when life felt overwhelming. Watching you grow, witnessing your resilience, your laughter, and your joy, has been the light that has guided me through the darkest times.

My hope for you is that you carry forward the lessons we've learned together. I hope you know that life won't always be easy, but that you are capable of facing whatever comes. I hope you trust in your own strength, in the power of faith, and in the importance of love. You are my legacy, and I am endlessly proud of the people you are becoming.

The End of One Chapter, the Beginning of Another

Writing this book has been an exercise in reflection, courage, and gratitude. It has allowed me to look back on all the moments that seemed impossible at the time, only to see how they shaped me, how they revealed strength I didn't know I had. This journey is far from over, but I carry forward with a heart full of hope, a soul rooted in faith, and the knowledge that no matter what happens, I have everything I need within me.

To everyone who has been part of this journey—whether in presence, in spirit, or through these pages—thank you. Thank you for listening, for understanding, for standing beside me in solidarity. May you find strength in your own journey, whatever it may look like, and may you always remember that you are not alone.

This is not the end, but a new beginning. With love, faith, and resilience, I move forward, ready to face whatever lies ahead, knowing that I am enough, and more than capable of whatever life brings.

With all my heart,
Latoya Glover

Author's Note

Writing this book has been a journey of reflection, gratitude, and purpose. As I put these words on the page, I was reminded of the strength that lies within us, even in moments when we feel we have nothing left to give. This book was born from my own experiences as a single mother—moments of triumph, times of doubt, and countless lessons learned along the way. My hope is that it serves as a source of encouragement and strength to any single mother who picks it up, reminding her that she is never truly alone.

To my children, Rayshawn, Anjel, and Asiah—you are the light of my life. Thank you for allowing me to be your mother and for giving my life a purpose deeper than I ever imagined. Because of you, I have grown and become a better, stronger woman. This journey hasn't always been easy, but it has been filled with love, resilience, and joy. I hope that as you grow, this book reminds you of everything we've been through together, and motivates you to carry forward the lessons we've learned as a family.

To every mother who may be reading this, please know that I understand your struggles, and admire your courage. If you ever need a listening ear, guidance, or simply someone to vent to, I am here. Don't hesitate to contact me at

. We may walk different paths, but we are all part of the same sisterhood of strength. Together, we are more resilient, more capable, and more extraordinary than we realize.

With love and faith,
Latoya Glover